CW01218733

SCIENCE MUSEUM
KIDS' HANDBOOK

WELCOME TO A WORLD OF SCIENTIFIC DISCOVERY!

CARLTON KIDS

SCIENCE FACT!
There are more than 15,000 items on display in the museum

The Science Museum is home to the world's greatest collection of science and technology exhibits.

THE AMAZING SCIENCE MUSEUM

For more than 100 years the Science Museum has brought the world of science and discovery to life with its amazing collection.

A visit really is a journey of scientific discovery, where you can find everything from George Stephenson's Rocket, the railway locomotive that started the steam age, through to the Pilot ACE computer that paved the way for today's high-tech computer age.

The Pilot ACE (short for Advanced Computing Engine) from 1950.

The Rocket started a transport revolution back in 1829.

A WORLD OF DISCOVERY

Right from its early days, the Science Museum has been the place to discover science in a hands-on way.

SCIENCE FACT!
Around 3 million people visit the Science Museum each year. That's enough to fill Wembley Stadium about 30 times!

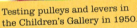

Testing pulleys and levers in the Children's Gallery in 1950.

Hands-on experiments and touch screens today.

YOUR KIDS' HANDBOOK

FUN AND GAMES

There are stacks of great games, puzzles and quizzes, plus cool experiments to try at home.

DISCOVER MORE

Your fact-packed *Handbook* lets you discover even more about science and inventions.

DID YOU KNOW?
By 2040, there could be 1,200 million cars on the world's roads.

STICKER FUN

Look out for spaces to add your stickers. Don't forget to add a sticker if you've spotted something in the Science Museum!

SEEN IT AT THE SCIENCE MUSEUM!

ADD YOUR STICKER HERE

POWER TO MOVE

For thousands of years people used their own muscle power or that of animals, such as horses, for travelling and working machinery. New power sources led to new inventions that made travel and work easier.

PEDAL POWER

If you've ever tried to cycle uphill, you'll know that it takes energy to get things moving! The first bicycles hit the streets about 150 years ago, but they looked a bit different to modern bikes.

BMX bikes were first developed in the 1970s.

1884 RUDGE 'ORDINARY' BICYCLE

This was a lighter, 'racing' version of the famous Penny Farthing or 'High Ordinary' bicycle.

1885 ROVER SAFETY BICYCLE

This design by John Kemp Starley was lower and more stable than Penny Farthing style bikes.

No bike chain – you pedalled the wheels directly here.

No gears – and no brakes either!

The rider had less distance to fall than on a Penny Farthing.

A bicycle chain links the pedals to the back wheel.

The two wheels were almost the same size!

The larger the front wheel, the further a bike moves with one turn of the pedals.

STEAM POWER

In the 1800s the discovery of steam power kick-started the Industrial Revolution and a transport revolution! Steam powered the machinery in cotton mills and factories, as well as trains and steamships.

2. The beam rocks up and down.

3. A connecting rod turns the flywheel round.

1. Steam moves the piston up and down.

1784 BEAM ENGINE

James Watt and Matthew Boulton's beam engine turned the up-and-down motion of a piston into rotary motion that could power other machines.

SEEN IT AT THE SCIENCE MUSEUM!

1829 ROCKET STEAM ENGINE

George Stephenson's Rocket won a steam engine race to run the first steam passenger railway between Liverpool and Manchester in 1829.

STEAMSHIP MAZE

Can you find a route across the waves for the giant steamship *SS Great Eastern*?

Start

Finish

The answer is at the back of the book.

PETROL POWER

In the 1850s a new fuel called petrol changed the world of transport. In 1885 the German inventor Karl Benz invented the Motorwägen – the first practical car to run on petrol.

KARL BENZ

1888 THE BENZ 1.5HP MOTOR CAR

The Benz 1.5hp is one of the oldest surviving cars in the UK.

Luckily I invented my car before they invented the traffic jam

Instead of a steering wheel, the driver used this handle.

There were seats for the driver and three passengers

The frame was made of steel tubes.

Wooden carriage-type wheels were used, with metal rims.

TRAFFIC LIGHT STICKER QUIZ

? Add a red sticker for FALSE or a green one for TRUE.

TRUE   FALSE

1. The Benz 1.5hp was the first production car in the world (that means it was not a one-off).

2. It had a top speed of more than 90km/h.

3. The first long-distance drive was made by Benz's wife, Bertha, who drove to visit her mum.

4. Traffic lights were invented in 1868 - in fact, before the car was invented!

The answers are at the back of the book.

HOW A PETROL ENGINE WORKS

A petrol engine burns petrol, using its explosive force to move pistons up and down. This vertical movement is changed into a circular motion that turns the wheels of a car.

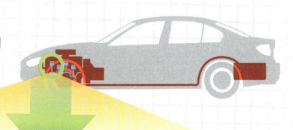

1 Each piston moves down inside a cylinder, sucking in in air and petrol. It's an explosive mix!

2 The piston moves up, squashing the petrol and air into a small space.

3 Bang! A spark explodes the air and petrol mixture, pushing the piston down.

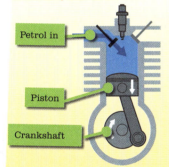

Petrol in

Piston

Crankshaft

Petrol and air

Piston moves down

Connecting rod

Crankshaft turns round

4 The piston moves up again pushing the waste gases out.

Exhaust gases pushed out

Piston moves up

MAD DOG II SOLAR POWERED CAR

This car uses the energy of sunlight instead of petrol! Could cars like this be the transport of the future?

ADD YOUR STICKER HERE

SEEN IT AT THE SCIENCE MUSEUM!

GREEN ENERGY

Burning coal, oil and gas can harm the environment and these fossil fuels will eventually run out. Scientists have invented ways to harness the power of the sun, wind and water too.

Turbine blades spin

WIND POWER

The wind turns the giant propellers of wind turbines to generate electricity. Sensors move the propeller blades to catch the wind.

WIND POWER

Rotation generates electricity

Electricity is moved to where it's needed through long metal cables on pylons like this.

SUNLIGHT

WATER POWER

Hydroelectric power stations use the water flowing through dams to generate electricity. Tidal barrages use the power of the tides as the sea flows in and out.

Solar energy is turned to electricity

SOLAR POWER

You may have spotted roofs that have been fitted with solar panels. These use the energy in sunlight to make electricity.

Turning turbines create electricity

WATER POWER

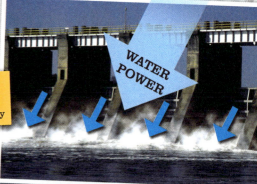

MAKE A WIND TURBINE

Make a model wind turbine to see
how wind power makes things turn.

EXPERIMENT ZONE

WHAT YOU NEED
• Paper • Scissors • Felt-tipped pen • Map pin • Plastic bead • Drinking straw

1

Fold a 10cm square of paper corner
to corner both ways to make diagonal
creases. Open it out again.

2

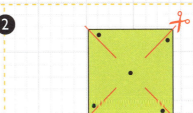

Mark dots in the places shown beside
the creases. Then cut two-thirds of the
way along the creases, as shown. Make
holes in the dots.

3

Fold over each corner with
a hole to the centre, then
carefully push the map pin
through all the holes.

4

Fit a bead onto the pin
and push it through the
top of a drinking straw.

5

Go outdoors and hold
your wind turbine up
to the wind and watch
what happens!

TOP TIP

If your wind turbine doesn't turn
well, wiggle the pin to make the
holes a bit bigger.

EXPERIMENT!

• Make bigger and smaller wind turbines.
  Which turns the fastest?
• Make wind turbines from thin and
  thick paper. Which turns best?
• Face into and away from the wind.
  Which way is best?

SPACE

For thousands of years, people looked up at the night sky and wondered what was out there. The work of those early stargazers continues with modern astronomers and space explorers.

ADD YOUR STICKER HERE

I spy... craters on the moon!

GALILEO GALILEI

WHAT IS SPACE ?

Space is vast, airless, silent and bitterly cold. The average temperature is -270°C, which is three times as cold as the lowest temperature ever recorded in Antarctica, the coldest place on Earth!

HOW DO WE KNOW WHATS IN SPACE ?

Thanks to astronomers such as Galileo Galilei. In 1609, he was first to look at the Moon through a telescope. He discovered that it had craters and ridges, invisible to the naked eye.

WHAT IS THE HUBBLE TELESCOPE ?

It's a space telescope that was launched into orbit around the Earth in 1990. It has taken more than half a million pictures of things in space.

HUBBLE TELESCOPE

URANUS

JUPITER

EARTH

SUN

MERCURY

VENUS

MARS

SATURN

NEPTUNE

HOW DO WE EXPLORE SPACE ?

Rockets and space shuttles have carried astronauts and scientists into space. They have orbited the Earth and even travelled to the Moon. Scientists have also sent robots and probes to distant planets to explore.

SEEN IT AT THE **SCIENCE MUSEUM!**

The Huygens probe landed on Titan, one of Saturn's moons in 2004 after a 7-year journey.

SOLAR SYSTEM SEARCH

Can you find all eight planets of our solar system in this word search puzzle?

V	S	Y	G	S	H	U	N
E	M	S	C	R	M	R	M
N	A	V	U	E	U	A	E
U	R	B	E	T	L	N	R
S	S	H	A	I	D	U	C
G	Q	S	R	P	W	S	U
N	E	P	T	U	N	E	R
B	E	A	H	J	F	H	Y

The answer is at the back of the book.

The Curiosity Rover is a robot exploring Mars.

SPACE EXPLORERS

Other than the Earth, the Moon is the only other place in space where humans have ever walked and explored.

TO THE MOON AND BACK

In May 1969, three astronauts successfully orbited the Moon in the cramped Apollo 10 Command Module and returned to Earth. It was a rehearsal for the Apollo 11 Moon landing in July 1969.

Apollo 10 astronauts, Eugene Cernan, Thomas Stafford and John Young.

APOLLO 10 COMMAND MODULE

ADD YOUR STICKER HERE

SEEN IT AT THE **SCIENCE MUSEUM!**

AMAZING MOON FACTS

The Moon is made of rock and dust. It has no light of its own, it just reflects sunlight.

In 1969, Apollo 11 went to the Moon and Neil Armstrong was the first person to set foot on it.

Because there's no wind or rain on the Moon, his footprints are still there today!

Only 12 people have ever walked on the Moon.

Saturn V rockets carried astronauts to the Moon. The journey took three days!

ROCKET SCIENCE!

WHAT YOU NEED
* An empty plastic milk bottle (the bigger the better) * Glue or sticky tape * Scissors

You need a lot of energy to beat Earth's gravity and travel into space. Rocket engines burn a mixture of fuel and oxygen, producing gas, smoke and flames as it blasts off into space.

Make your own rocket and experiment with forces to launch it into the air! Tear out this page and follow the instructions on the other side.

Decorate this side with stickers and add yourself looking out of the window!

Glue here

Cut along this line

INSTRUCTIONS

1 Cut out your rocket along the solid pink lines. Roll it into a cone, overlapping the shaded area. Use glue to stick it in place.

2 Stand the bottle upright (with the top off) and put your rocket over the top.

3 Squeeze the bottle by clapping your hands together.

4 Watch your rocket blast off into the air!

HOW IT WORKS

Rapidly squeezing the air out of the bottle, provides the force to temporarily overcome gravity and lift your rocket into the air.

SCIENCE FACT!
Thousands of satellites orbit the Earth, beaming TV signals, phone calls and images around the world.

EXPERIMENT!

- Try one litre and two litre bottles to find out which makes your rocket travel further.
- Add some weight to your rocket e.g. some plasticine inside. How does being heavier affect your rocket?

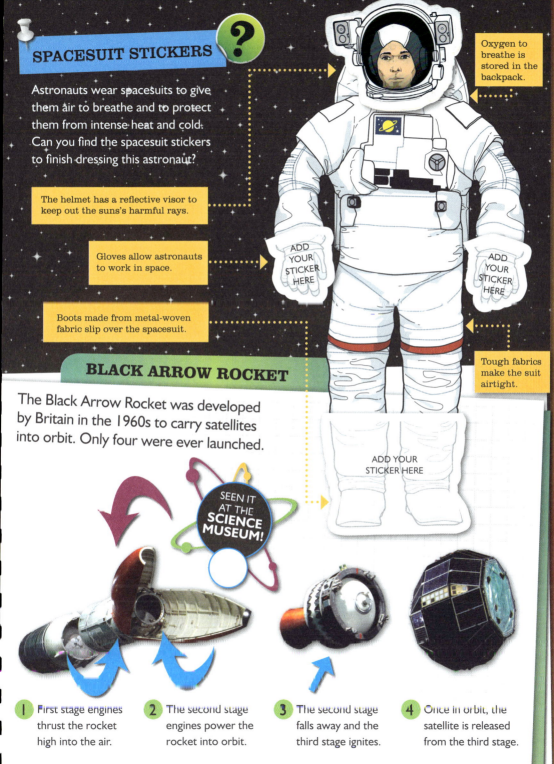

SPACESUIT STICKERS

Astronauts wear spacesuits to give them air to breathe and to protect them from intense heat and cold. Can you find the spacesuit stickers to finish dressing this astronaut?

Oxygen to breathe is stored in the backpack.

The helmet has a reflective visor to keep out the suns's harmful rays.

Gloves allow astronauts to work in space.

Boots made from metal-woven fabric slip over the spacesuit.

Tough fabrics make the suit airtight.

ADD YOUR STICKER HERE

ADD YOUR STICKER HERE

ADD YOUR STICKER HERE

BLACK ARROW ROCKET

The Black Arrow Rocket was developed by Britain in the 1960s to carry satellites into orbit. Only four were ever launched.

SEEN IT AT THE **SCIENCE MUSEUM!**

1 First stage engines thrust the rocket high into the air.

2 The second stage engines power the rocket into orbit.

3 The second stage falls away and the third stage ignites.

4 Once in orbit, the satellite is released from the third stage.

FLIGHT

Many inventors have looked for ways to fly through the sky like birds. Check out these pioneering flying machines that made it off the ground and into history!

1783 FIRST HOT AIR BALLOON

The French Montgolfier brothers made this hot-air balloon in 1783. It flew over Paris with a cockerel, a duck and a sheep on board.

Quack Quack

1893 FIRST GLIDER

German engineer, Otto Lilienthal built and flew the first piloted gliders. In 1893, he glided almost 230m.

IT'S A FACT!
500 years ago, Leonardo da Vinci invented more than 60 flying machines. Sadly not one made it off the drawing board!

1903 WRIGHT FLYER 1

Made by the American Wright brothers, this aircraft, Flyer 1, made the first ever powered flight. Its best flight on the day lasted 59 seconds.

FLYER 1

1919 FIRST ATLANTIC FLIGHT

In 1919, Alcock and Brown were the first to fly non-stop across the Atlantic. Their journey in a Vickers Vimy biplane took 16 hours and 27 minutes.

VICKERS VIMY

SEEN IT AT THE **SCIENCE MUSEUM!**

1930 DE HAVILLAND GYPSY MOTH

In 1930 Amy Johnson became the first woman to fly solo from Britain to Australia. She made the 18,000km journey in a Gypsy Moth biplane.

AMY JOHNSON

1931 SUPERMARINE S.6B SEAPLANE

In 1931, this seaplane was the first aircraft to fly faster than 400mph (644km/h). It had floats for take off and landing on water.

ADD YOUR STICKER HERE

THE JET AGE

Aircraft with propellors could not fly very fast or high.
Frank Whittle's invention of the jet engine led to modern
jet airliners and supersonic fighter planes.

SEEN IT AT THE SCIENCE MUSEUM!

1941 FIRST BRITISH JET PLANE

This Gloster-Whittle
E28/39 was the first
British plane with a jet
engine. It made its first
flight in 1941.

GLOSTER-WHITTLE E28/39

HOW A JET ENGINE WORKS

A jet engine burns compressed air and fuel,
creating hot gases to power a jet plane.

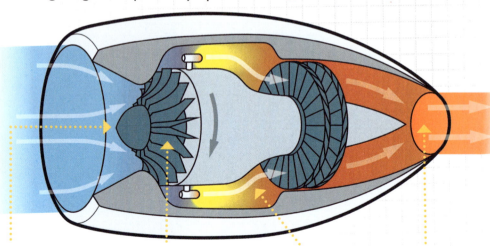

1 Huge rotating fan
blades draw air into
the engine.

2 Spinning blades compress
the air and pump it into the
combustion chamber.

3 Fuel burns in the
combustion chamber
producing hot gases.

4 Hot gases blast out
and thrust the aircraft
forward.

DESIGN A PLANE

Draw an amazing new plane of the future here. What shape will it be? What will power it through the sky?

CONCORDE

FASTEST JET EVER

The Lockheed Blackbird holds the record for the world's fastest jet plane. Its top speed is more than 3,200km/h.

FASTEST PASSENGER PLANE

Concorde was the fastest passenger plane in service, travelling at more than 2,000km/h, or twice the speed of sound. It holds the record for the fastest flight from London to New York – 2 hours, 52 minutes and 59 seconds!

LOCKHEED BLACKBIRD

PAPER PLANES

Aeroplane inventors make models of their planes to test how they fly. You can do the same!

1

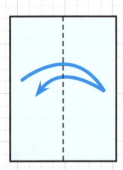

Fold a sheet of paper in half to make a crease. Open it out again.

2

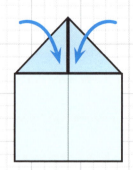

Fold in the top left and right corners into the centre crease.

3

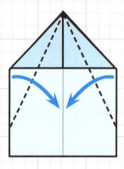

Fold in both sides towards the centre crease again.

4

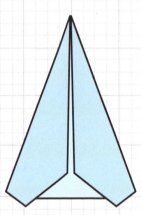

The plane should now look like this. Turn it over.

5

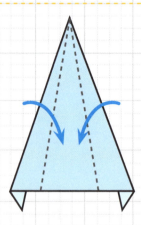

Fold both sides to the centre crease.

6

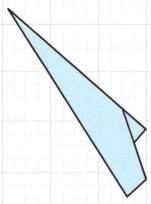

Bend the whole plane in half, along the centre crease.

HOW A WING WORKS

The different speeds of airflow over a wing create lift.

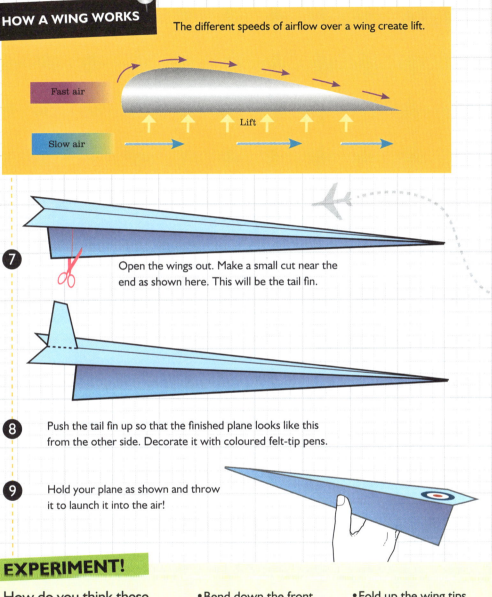

Fast air

Lift

Slow air

7 Open the wings out. Make a small cut near the end as shown here. This will be the tail fin.

8 Push the tail fin up so that the finished plane looks like this from the other side. Decorate it with coloured felt-tip pens.

9 Hold your plane as shown and throw it to launch it into the air!

EXPERIMENT!

How do you think these ideas will affect the way your plane flies? Try them out and see if you are correct!

- Bend down the front of your plane.
- Attach a paperclip to the front to add weight.

- Fold up the wing tips.
- Fold down the wing tips.

MODERN MATERIALS

Once people only had natural materials, such as wood, leather and wool to make things. The modern world uses man-made materials too, including glass, steel, nylon, polyester and plastic.

Plastic is fantastic!

1856 PARKESINE

Alexander Parkes made the first man-made plastic using cotton dissolved in acid and solvent. He called it Parkesine. It could be heated and moulded into different shapes, but Parkesine was expensive to make and easily caught fire.

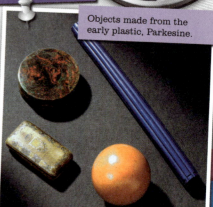

Objects made from the early plastic, Parkesine.

PLASTIC FILE

Plastic is one of the most useful man-made materials. It can be moulded into any shape and is light, strong, waterproof, easy to clean and almost unbreakable.

• There are many more than 50 different types of plastic. Some are bendy and lightweight, others are strong and rigid.

• Most plastics are made from oil.

• See if you can spot a number on the base of a plastic bottle or container. It tells you what kind of plastic it is made of. PET, number 1, is one of the most common plastics and is recyclable.

1909 BAKELITE

Bakelite was another early man-made plastic, named after its inventor the chemist Leo Baekeland. It was described as a 'material of 1000 uses' and is still used to make things, including chess pieces.

ADD YOUR STICKER HERE

The case of this 1950s TV uses Bakelite instead of wood.

1973 PLASTIC BOTTLE

Nathaniel Wyeth invented the plastics drink bottle. Tough enough for fizzy drinks, it was cheaper than glass and harder to break. More than 50 billion bottles are now made every year!

On average, everyone in the UK uses 168 plastic bottles a year.

SPOT THE PLASTIC!

Tick the everyday objects that are made of plastic.

1

2

3

4

5

6

7

8

The answers are at the back of the book.

TALKING TECHNOLOGY

Today, mobile phone calls, texts and emails put us instantly in touch and play a big part in modern life. The telephone has come a long way since it was first invented!

1876 THE FIRST PHONE CALL

Alexander Graham Bell made the first phone call, using an electrical speech machine that he had invented. On 10 March 1876 he made a call to the next room, saying, "Mr. Watson, come here. I want to see you."

I think I'll call my new invention the telephone.

ALEXANDER GRAHAM BELL

BELL TELEPHONE

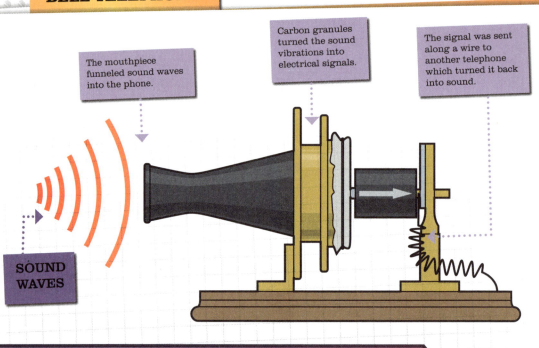

The mouthpiece funneled sound waves into the phone.

Carbon granules turned the sound vibrations into electrical signals.

The signal was sent along a wire to another telephone which turned it back into sound.

SOUND WAVES

FAMOUS PHONE CALL

Follow the tangled phone wires to reveal which famous person Bell demonstrated his telephone to.

ALBERT EINSTEIN

QUEEN VICTORIA

THOMAS EDISON

SEEN IT AT THE SCIENCE MUSEUM!

The answer is at the back of the book.

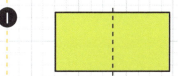

EXPERIMENT ZONE

Sound is vibrating air. Try this experiment to feel and hear how vibrations become sound waves.

1

Cut a piece of thin paper into a rectangle about 5cm x 3cm. Fold it in half.

2

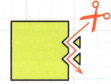

Snip out two small triangles along the fold.

3

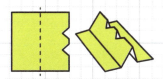

Fold back the edges either side of the fold like this.

4

Hold the flat edges against your lips as shown and blow.

INFORMATION AGE

The invention of the computer changed the way we communicate and access information. With email, the internet and smart phones, our modern world is a place of instant information, sounds and pictures.

```
0110101110101000
1000011101010101
1000011010000000
1010100000011001
0000111010101010
0100010101010110
```

MECHANICAL COMPUTER

An inventor called Charles Babbage drew up plans for mechanical computers more than 150 years ago. None were built during Babbage's lifetime, but his ideas led to modern computers.

Behind all the emails, websites and games is a computer language made of just zeros and ones!

The Science Museum built Babbage's Difference Engine computer – and it worked!

A computer language is named ADA after me!

THE FIRST COMPUTER PROGRAMMER

Ada Lovelace worked with Charles Babbage. She was the first person to work out the principles of computer programming, so she's often called the world's first programmer.

COLOSSAL COMPUTERS

Colossus was a type of early electronic computer that was built to crack German military codes during World War II. Each Colossus computer filled a large room.

Colossus with computer operators from the Women's Royal Naval Service.

PERSONAL COMPUTERS

The first personal computers for use in the home were developed in the 1970s. Most were built by people as a hobby, including this Apple I, which was built in 1976.

The Apple I Computer, complete with keyboard and screen.

COMPUTER WORD SEARCH

Can you find these computer words in the grid below?

EMAIL
KEYBOARD
PROGRAM
MOUSE
WEBSITE
LAPTOP
MICROCHIP
SOFTWARE
APP
DOWNLOAD

The answer is at the back of the book.

M	O	U	S	E	L	A	R	A	D
B	W	P	R	O	G	R	A	M	O
E	E	M	A	I	L	F	D	G	W
A	B	D	S	L	W	R	Y	L	N
F	S	B	J	T	A	M	O	A	L
M	I	C	R	O	C	H	I	P	O
Z	T	P	B	U	T	K	I	T	A
J	E	Y	C	A	P	P	B	O	D
U	E	D	H	W	D	K	R	P	I
K	Q	S	O	F	T	W	A	R	E

MEDICAL MARVELS

Medical inventions and discoveries help doctors to find out what's wrong with people and to make them better. It is much easier to prevent and cure illnesses now than it was in the past.

1798 THE FIRST VACCINATION

English country doctor Edward Jenner invented a vaccination that prevented people from catching a deadly disease called smallpox. His idea caught on and now this disease has been completely wiped out!

Prevention is better than a cure!

EDWARD JENNER

The word vaccine comes from 'vacca' the Latin word for cow.

Moo! I helped to make medical history.

MEDICAL NOTES

Dairymaids who caught a similar, milder disease called cowpox from cows, didn't catch smallpox.

Jenner used pus from cowpox spots to vaccinate people and prevent them catching smallpox.

The cow with cowpox that led to the first vaccine was called Blossom.

People mocked Jenner and thought cowpox vaccinations would turn people into cows!

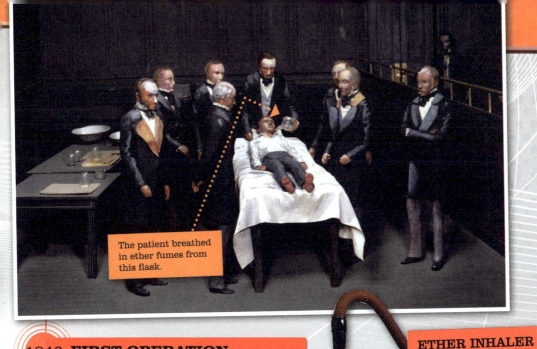

The patient breathed in ether fumes from this flask.

1846 FIRST OPERATION USING ANAESTHETIC

Just imagine how terrible it was to have an operation before anaesthetics were discovered! The first operation that used anaesthetic to stop the patient feeling any pain was carried out at the Massachusetts Hospital in Boston, USA.

ETHER INHALER 1847-1848

Patients breathed in fumes of an anaesthetic called ether through this mouthpiece.

1866 CLINICAL THERMOMETER

The thermometer was invented in 1714 by a German scientist called Daniel Fahrenheit, but they weren't widely used by doctors until Thomas Allbutt invented this pocket-sized version.

DID YOU KNOW?
Normal body temperature is 37.5°C. Anything higher or lower than this could mean that you're ill

Mercury in the bulb expands as it gets hotter and rises up the tube.

The patient's temperature is read off the scale

MORE MEDICAL MARVELS

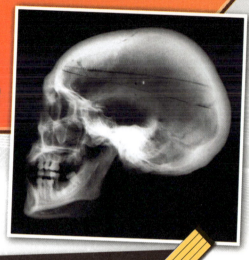

1895 X-RAYS ARE DISCOVERED

X-rays let doctors see inside a living body. They pass through skin and muscles, but not bone. Bones show up white on an X-ray picture, so that doctors can see if any are broken.

X-RAY PICTURE PUZZLE

Colour in the shapes with an X to create your own X-ray picture!

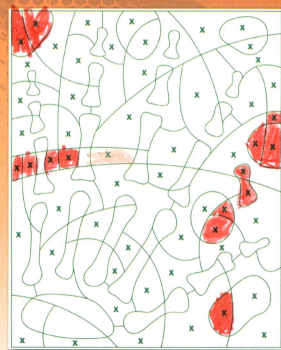

WILHELM RÖNTGEN

I called my new rays X for unknown!

X-rays were accidentally discovered by the German scientist Wilhelm Röntgen. He found that strange rays from an electrical tube in one of his experiments showed up on a photograph.

The answer is at the back of the book.

1928 THE FIRST ANTIBIOTICS

In 1928, Alexander Fleming made a lucky discovery. He found that a mould growing in his laboratory could kill harmful bacteria. This led to the first antibiotic medicines.

In the 1940s, chemist Dorothy Hodgkin used X-ray photographs to work out the structure of this first antibiotic, which helped in the development of similar medicines.

ALEXANDER FLEMING

DOROTHY HODGKIN

Dorothy Hodgkin later received the Nobel Prize for Chemistry.

PILL PUZZLER!

Copy the letters from the pills into the matching coloured boxes to reveal the name of the first antibiotic.

L E I P N C

The answer is at the back of the book.

1950 BINAURAL STETHOSCOPE

A stethoscope lets doctors hear sounds inside the body, including the heart and lungs. René Laennecc invented the first stethoscope in 1816, but later versions, such as this stethoscope from 1950, were flexible and had two earpieces.

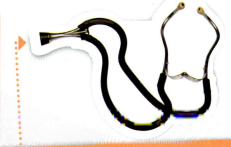

Sound travels from the patient's chest, through the rubber tubes and into the earpieces.

Messy MEDICAL HISTORY

Thanks to medical science we know what causes many illnesses and know about healthy eating and exercise. In the past medical ideas were quite different, which led to some extreme cures like these!

BAD BLOOD

Until a few hundred years ago, people thought that some illnesses were caused by too much 'bad blood'. To get rid of this blood doctors bled a patient, or attached blood-sucking leeches - eek!

This picture shows a patient ready for blood-letting!

DID YOU KNOW?

Sometimes, as many as 20 leeches were used at the same time when bleeding a patient.

LEECH COUNT

How many leeches can you count in this doctor's leech jar?

Live leeches were kept in jars, ready for use.

ADD YOUR STICKER HERE

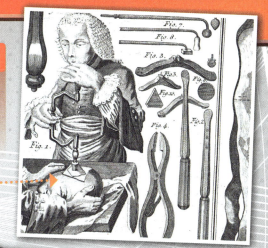

HEADACHE?

Nowadays we have medicines called painkillers, but in the past drilling a hole in a person's skull was thought to be a cure for bad headaches or mental upsets.

Drilling a hole in someone's head was called 'trepanning'.

This cranial trephine removed a circle of bone in someone's skull - ouch!

FEELING SICK?

Giving people medicines that made them throw up or have diarrhoea was once thought to clean out the body. From the look on this man's face, the cure must have been pretty nasty!

Bowl to collect vomit – yuk!

The medicine to make you sick was called an emetic.

WHAT IS IT?

People have invented all kinds of medical kit, but what is this?

a) a foot stretcher
b) an exercise chair
c) a back massager

The answer is at the back of the book.

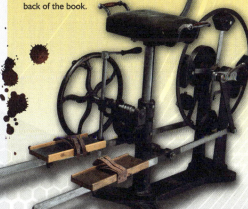

FUTURE SCIENCE

The science and inventions of the future are being made now, with people developing robots, new forms of transport and high-tech gadgets. Just imagine what the future will be like!

SPACE TOURISM

Space may well become a top holiday destination in your lifetime. New rocket planes and mini-shuttles are being developed to take passengers on a trip that is truly out of this world!

SpaceShip Two will launch from the back of an aeroplane using rockets.

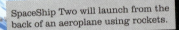

Virgin Galactic's SpaceShip Two is designed to take passengers into space.

These wings fold down on return to Earth for a landing like an aeroplane.

Each bulb holds many small LEDs that produce light.

BRIGHT IDEAS

Closer to home, could LED bulbs be the lightbulbs of the future? They are long-lasting, have no glass tubes to break and are more energy efficient than standard low energy lightbulbs.

LED is short for Light Emitting Diode. These convert electricity into light.

FUN SCIENCE TEST

Inventors come up with more than 200,000 new inventions each year. Maybe you could be a great inventor like Thomas Edison? Try our fun science test to find out!

THOMAS EDISON

I find out what the world needs, then I proceed to invent.

Thomas Edison made many inventions, including the electric lamp and early cinema and sound recording devices.

Start

Are you always asking questions?

Yes | **No**

Do friends ask you to help to solve their problems?

No → Are you a bit of a dreamer? ← **Yes** Does making a mess bother you much?

Yes | **Yes** | **No** | **No**

Are you tidy and organised? **No** → Are you always after quick results?

Are you good at making things with your hands?

Yes | **No** | **Yes** | **No**

Scientist
You think logically and could be making amazing scientific discoveries one day!

Inventor
You're very creative, with an eye for how ideas can lead to practical inventions.

Mad Scientist!
Perhaps you have a scary laugh and are planning to rule the world?

FUTURE HOMES

Scientists think that by the year 2100 our planet could be between 2°C and 6°C hotter. This will lead to glaciers and the polar ice caps melting – sea levels will rise and flooding will become more common.

As glaciers and ice sheets have melted over the last century, sea level has risen up to 25cm.

GLOBAL WARMING

Many scientists believe that an increase in gases like carbon dioxide in the atmosphere is trapping too much heat and causing global temperature rises.

NEW IDEAS

As the planet gets warmer we'll have to change how we live. For example, higher sea levels will flood low-lying land, so we may have to rethink where we build our homes and how they are designed.

With less land we might build homes that float on the sea like this.

HOUSE OF THE FUTURE

What will our homes look like in the future?
Draw your idea for a house of the future below.

Where and how will you build your house,
in order to avoid flooding?

In a tree?

On stilts?

WHAT MATERIALS WILL YOU USE?

Wood
Stone
Plastic
Brick
Glass
Straw

ANSWERS

Start

Finish

Page 8 Traffic Light Sticker Quiz

1 True, **2 False** - its top speed was 13km/h,
3 True, **4 True**

Page 11 Solar System Search

V	S	Y	G	S	H	U	N
E	M	S	C	R	M	R	M
N	A	V	U	E	U	A	E
U	R	B	E	T	L	N	R
S	S	H	A	I	D	U	C
G	Q	S	R	P	W	S	U
N	E	P	T	U	N	E	R
B	E	A	H	J	F	H	Y

Page 23 Spot the Plastic!

2, 3, 5 and 7 are all made with plastic.

Page 25 Famous Phone Call

Alexander Graham Bell demonstrated his telephone to Queen Victoria at her house on the Isle of Wight in 1878.

Page 27 Computer Word Search

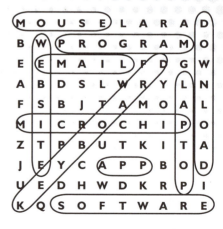

M	O	U	S	E	L	A	R	A	D
B	W	P	R	O	G	R	A	M	O
E	E	M	A	I	L	F	D	G	W
A	B	D	S	L	W	R	Y	L	N
F	S	B	J	T	A	M	O	A	L
M	I	C	R	O	C	H	I	P	O
Z	T	P	B	U	T	K	I	T	A
J	E	Y	C	A	P	P	B	O	D
U	E	D	H	W	D	K	R	P	I
K	Q	S	O	F	T	W	A	R	E

Page 30 X-ray Picture Puzzle

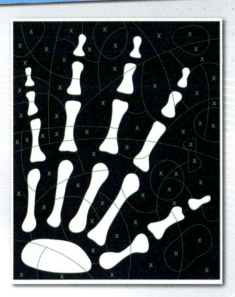

Page 31 Pill Puzzler

Penicillin

Page 32 Leech Count

12 leeches

Page 33 What is it?

An exercise chair.

Gatefold Science Museum Search

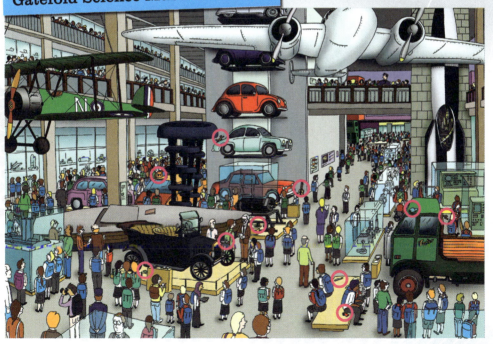

Inspired by the Science Museum's amazing collection? Try drawing your own invention here!

ISBN: 978-1-78097-346-3

Produced exclusively for SCMG Enterprises Ltd. Science Museum ® SCMG and designs/images © SCMG. Every purchase supports the museum. www.sciencemuseum.org.uk

The Science Museum is the most popular destination for science, technology and engineering in the UK. Offering visitors of all ages an incredible collection of objects, both historical and cutting edge, as well as contemporary science learning and debate, we help make sense of the science that shapes our lives and gives inspiration to scientists of the future.

The publishers would like to thank the following sources for their kind permission to reproduce the pictures in this book.Thinkstockphotos.co.uk: p4, p8, p11, p23, p34, p36, p37. iStockphoto.com: p16. NASA: /JPL-Caltech: p11. Virgin Galactic p34. Don Farrall/Getty Images: cover. Bletchley Park Trust/SSPL: p27. All other photos: © Science & Society Picture Library (SSPL)

Every effort has been made to acknowledge correctly and contact the source and/or copyright holder of each picture and Carlton Books Limited apologises for any unintentional errors or omissions, which will be corrected in future editions of this book.

Illustrations: Peter Liddiard, William Ings.